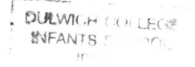

D0655891

The Life of Plants

Plant Classification

Richard & Louise Spilsbury

Heinemann
LIBRARY

H **www.heinemann.co.uk**
Visit our website to find out more information about **Heinemann Library** books.

To order:
☎ Phone 44 (0) 1865 888066
▤ Send a fax to 44 (0) 1865 314091
▢ Visit the Heinemann Bookshop at www.heinemann.co.uk to browse our catalogue and order online.

First published in Great Britain by Heinemann Library,
Halley Court, Jordan Hill, Oxford OX2 8EJ
a division of Harcourt Education
Heinemann is a registered trademark of Harcourt Education Ltd.

Designed by Macwiz
Illustrated by Jeff Edwards
Originated by Ambassador Litho Ltd
Printed by Wing King Tong, Hong Kong

ISBN 0 431 11883 3
06 05 04 03 02
10 9 8 7 6 5 4 3 2 1

British Library Cataloguing in Publication Data
Spilsbury, Louise
      Plant classification. - (Life of plants)
      1. Botany - Classification - Juvenile literature
      I. Title II. Spilsbury, Richard, 1963-
      580.1'2

Acknowledgements
The Publishers would like to thank the following for permission to reproduce photographs: Corbis: pp5, 6, 14, 15, 24, 34, 37; Flpa: pp10, 31; Holt Studios: pp4, 7, 8, 13, 16, 19, 20, 21, 22, 23, 25, 28, 32, 33, 39; Oxford Scientific Films: pp12, 17, 18, 26, 27, 30, 35, 38; Photodisc: p29; Science Photo Library: p36; Hemera: flower motif

Cover photographs reproduced with permission of A-Z Botanical Collection Ltd, Holt Studios, Natural Visions

Our thanks to Andrew Solway for his comments in the preparation of this book.

Every effort has been made to contact copyright holders of any material reproduced in this book. Any omissions will be rectified in subsequent printings if notice is given to the Publisher.

Contents

Any words appearing in the text in bold, **like this**, are explained in the glossary.

A plant may be called different things in different countries, so every type of plant has a Latin name that can be recognized anywhere in the world. Latin names are made of two words – the first is the genus (general group) a plant belongs to and the second is its species (specific) name. Latin plant names are given in brackets throughout this book.

What is classification?

Ever since humans first walked the Earth, they have tried to make sense of the world around them. Faced with a multitude of different plants and animals, it helps to be able to recognize and name what you can see, but also to understand how similar it is to something else. This is the essence of classification – grouping together living things according to characteristics that they share.

Sometimes the similarities between **organisms** are obvious – all elephants are large grey animals with a trunk and clearly belong in the same group. At other times, similarities are few – an elephant and a daisy clearly belong to different groups.

◄ When we classify a tree as an oak, we are not only describing its leaf shape and acorns. We are also saying that it is similar to other oak trees.

Ancestors

If you have red hair it is probably because your parents or **ancestors** had red hair. The reason many plants have shared features is that they have the same ancestors. All of the plants on Earth today have ancestors that first existed many millions of years ago. So, an important part of classification is telling the story of what happened in the past. However, like any story, not everyone tells it in the same way.

History of classification

The first humans on Earth probably classified plants as good or bad to eat, and animals as safe or dangerous to approach. Information like this would have been vital. People needed to know which animals to hunt and which might hunt them, which berries they could eat safely and which might poison them, so they could feed themselves and their families. They may also have grouped organisms into those of similar shape or colour.

From Aristotle to Linnaeus

The Ancient Greek thinker Aristotle lived over 2000 years ago. He was important in the history of classification because he worked out the main differences between animals and plants. Back then only a thousand or so different types of organisms were known. Centuries of study and observation followed in which other scientists from many countries classified more and more organisms. By working out similarities and differences between living things, they could also divide them into groups. In the 18th century, a Swedish scientist called Carl von Linné (Linnaeus) worked out a way of classifying all organisms. It is his system of classification that is the basis for the one used around the world today.

◄ Carl von Linné, known throughout the world as Linnaeus.

Name calling

Today, as in Linnaeus's time, there are lots of different names for the same plants in the different countries around the world. What is called a daisy in England is called margherita in Italy. So when people talked or wrote to each other about plants they often got confused.

Linnaeus's double-name system

To solve this problem, Linnaeus decided that each plant (or animal) should have a double name that could be used all over the world. He chose to write these double names in Latin, because this language was understood in most countries at this time.

In this double or Latin name system, the first name is the **genus** (general group) to which the plant or animal belongs and the second name describes the **species** (specific group). For example, daisy is *Bellis perennis*. *Bellis* tells us the genus, the group of plants to which the daisy belongs. Other plants with similar features also have that same first name. *Perennis* is the species name. Only plants and animals of the same species can **reproduce** together, so only two daisies of the same species can breed together successfully in the wild.

◄ The genus name for maple is *Acer*. There are about 200 trees and shrubs in the *Acer* genus. Each has its own species name – red maple is *Acer rubrum*.

Names with a story to tell

The names used in Linnaeus's system often say something about the way the plants look or grow. For example, *Campanula* means bell-shaped in Latin and is the name for a genus of plants with bell-shaped flowers. The Latin name for spiked bellflower is *Campanula spicata* – *spicata* means spiked. The bearded bellflower is also in the genus *Campanula*, but has the species name *barbata*, meaning bearded.

Clovers usually have three leaves so they belong to the genus *Trifolium* – *tri* means three and *folium* means leaf. It can be fun to guess what plant names mean. Some examples are *odorata*, which means the plant has a smell or odour, *vulgaris*, which means the plant is common (or vulgar), and *splendifera*, which means the plant is showy or splendid.

Most of us still use common names a lot of the time when we talk to each other about plants. However, it is good to know there is a universal naming system we can use to avoid any confusion!

▲ Bearded bellflower (*Campanula barbata*).

Naming today

Scientists today use special equipment to tell plant species apart. They can compare the **genes** of organisms to help classify them. It is big news when scientists find new species, so large international committees check that it really is a new species and decide on new names.

The kingdoms of life

Giving an **organism** a name that distinguishes it from all other organisms is one part of classification. To make further sense of life on Earth it is useful to group **organisms** together that have certain things in common. These things may be to do with the way the organisms **reproduce** or feed, or what bits they have inside the **cells** that make up their bodies.

All of the organisms across the world can be divided into five large groups called **kingdoms**. The organisms in one kingdom are more similar to each other than they are to organisms in the other kingdoms. Plants and animals are the two best-known kingdoms.

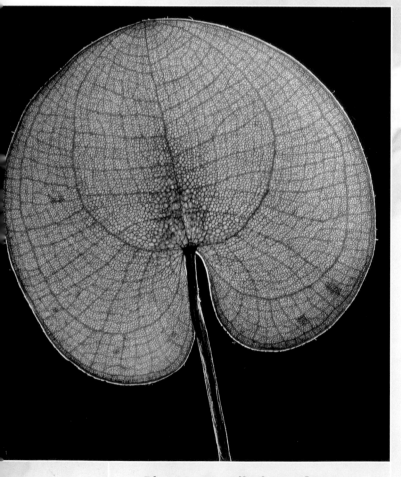

▲ Plants are called **producers** because they produce their own food. Photosynthesis occurs in their leaves.

Plant producers

Take a look at a tree and then yourself. It is pretty obvious how a plant is different to an animal! You move, it cannot; you have arms and legs, it has a trunk and branches. However, the single most remarkable thing that distinguishes plants from other living things is that they produce their own food inside their bodies. They do this using the process of **photosynthesis**. Photosynthesis is a way of trapping **energy** from the sun, which can be used to convert water and **carbon dioxide** (a gas in the air) into sugars and **oxygen**.

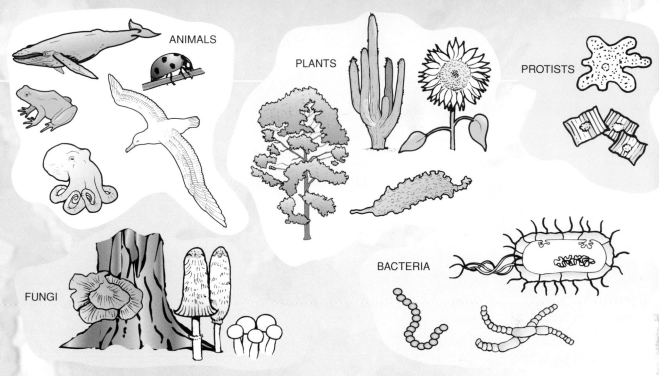

ANIMALS

PLANTS

PROTISTS

FUNGI

BACTERIA

▲ The five kingdoms of life.

Animal consumers

All animals need to eat some kind of food to survive, but animals cannot make their own food within themselves as plants do. They are **consumers**. They consume (eat) plants or the animals that eat plants. This means that plants, either directly or indirectly, are the source of all the food animals rely on to survive.

The other three kingdoms

The other living things on Earth are neither plants nor animals. They make up three further kingdoms. Many **fungi** may look a bit like plants but they make up a separate kingdom that contains organisms such as mushrooms and toadstools.

The remaining two kingdoms are made up of organisms you can only see using a microscope. They are single **cells** or groups of identical cells joined together. **Bacteria** are found in the air, soil and water. **Protists**, such as diatoms, live in water and form part of sea **plankton**.

Expanding kingdoms

So far, more than 1.75 million different species have been identified in the world. More are being discovered all the time. It is unlikely that many new large animals or plants will be found, but there are probably many undiscovered insects, bacteria and protists out there. The total number of different species could be nearer 13 million!

9

Within the plant kingdom

The plant **kingdom** contains **organisms** as different as mosses and cacti. It is useful to divide the plant kingdom into smaller groups that have certain things in common in order to study and discuss them. One way of grouping plants is to do with the way they take in water and **nutrients** – whether they are **vascular** or **nonvascular**.

▲ A vascular plant like this bamboo can grow tall, as its vessels carry the water it needs from its roots to leaves that are metres away.

What are vascular plants?

The majority of plants on Earth are vascular. They have vessels or tubes inside their **roots**, **stems** and leaves, which are connected together – a bit like the network of pipes in your home that brings water to your sink or bath. Some tubes in vascular plants carry water and nutrients from the roots to the other parts of the plant. These vessels are called **xylem**. Other tubes carry sugar made in the leaves by **photosynthesis** to other parts of the plant. These vessels are called **phloem**.

How do nonvascular plants work?

Nonvascular plants have no tubes to transport water and nutrients. They tend to live in damp places near the ground where all parts of their bodies can absorb (take in) what they need, so they rarely grow as tall as vascular plants.

Plant divisions

The world of plants is usually divided into five smaller groups or divisions. Members of each division **reproduce** in a similar way or have similar structures. For instance, plants are put in one division or another depending on whether they reproduce by **seeds** or not, or whether their seeds grow in **cones** or flowers.

Two of the divisions contain nonvascular plants. The first is algae, which includes water plants such as kelp. The second is mosses and liverworts, small green plants that live in damp places.

The three remaining divisions are vascular. One is ferns and their relatives. Clubmosses and horsetails are grouped with ferns because, although they don't resemble ferns, they have much in common with them. The second vascular division is the conifers, containing plants such as fir, pine and redwood, which bear their seeds in cones. Conifers are grouped with their close relatives, the cycads and ginkgoes. The final vascular division is flowering plants. Although their variety in shape and size is astonishing, flowering plant **species** are grouped together because they all use flowers to reproduce with.

VASCULAR PLANTS	NONVASCULAR PLANTS
Flowering plants Seeds, flowers	**Algae** Spores
Conifers Seeds, cones	**Mosses and liverworts** Spores
Ferns, clubmosses and horsetails Spores	

◄ **This chart shows how the plant kingdom is divided into five divisions. There are more flowering plants on Earth than any other kind of plant. Nine out of ten (90 per cent) of plant species are flowering plants.**

Nonvascular plants

What are algae?

Algae are thought to be the **ancestors** of all land plants. Algae are often described as simple plants. Some are made up of only one **cell**, or several very similar cells in a chain or thread. Other larger types have large leaf-like **fronds**. Some algae can only be seen under a microscope, but others can grow to many tens of metres in length.

▲ The water that algae grow in provides support and most of what they need to make their own food.

Algae are **nonvascular** plants and do not have leaves, **stems** or **roots**. All algae live in water or in moist places, where any part of their bodies can absorb (take in) what they need. Living in water also helps keep the shape of algae. Fronds and threads float in water – often with the help of in-built waterwings – allowing each part of the plant to absorb the sunlight it needs for **photosynthesis**.

Slippery customers

If you have ever walked on a beach at low tide you will have noticed how rocks covered in seaweed are slippery to walk on. This is because seaweed – algae that live in or by the sea – are covered in slime. Many algae out of water can lose water by **evaporation**, caused by the heat of the sun or the blowing wind. They make slime that forms a second skin on their fronds to help prevent water loss.

The danger of algal blooms

Single-celled algae can **reproduce** very quickly where there are extra nutrients in the water, often as a result of **pollution**. These gigantic increases in population are called algal blooms. The blooms soon begin to use up the **oxygen** in the water. Without oxygen, the animals and other plants in the water die.

Algae do not need roots, because all their parts absorb the **nutrients** they need straight from the water they live in. However, many seaweeds need to grow on particular parts of the seashore so that rough waves or strong sunlight do not damage them. For this reason, they grow **holdfasts** or suckers – which often look like roots – to grip the rocks.

New algae

The simplest, single-celled algae produce new algae by dividing into two identical cells. Larger algae produce **spores**, which are small parcels of **cells**. The spores form inside special areas on the fronds. Some spores produced by algae have very tough skins that can protect the cells inside from cold, heat and drought. In the right conditions – often when the water gets warmer – the cells in each spore can divide and grow into a new, microscopic plant. The new plant can produce male or female **sex cells**. If these are brought together by movements in the water, the **fertilized** female cell can grow into a new spore-producing plant.

Types of algae

If someone is asked to name a type of algae they usually say seaweed. There are actually around 12,000 different **species** of algae and only about half of them live in the sea.

Algae come in many different colours: yellow-green, golden-brown, green, brown and red. Most green algae live in pond and lake water or around their edges. Some live in seawater, but others live on land, or damp surfaces, such as old gates. In South America, tiny green algae live on slow-moving three-toed sloths, giving them the greenish tinge that helps them hide in the trees! Green algae are often delicate plants, one or a few **cells** across, but one of the most familiar types, sea lettuce, can be 30 centimetres long.

Living in harmony

Lichen are **organisms** that look a bit like plants, but they are actually a partnership of algae and **fungi**! Each type of organism needs the other to live. The algae make sugar by **photosynthesis** to feed themselves but also the fungi, which provide shelter and collect water for the algae. The two organisms grow together and are so closely entwined and therefore hard to classify that scientists gave them their own separate name – lichen.

◄ These are tiny algae that float in the sea. They are known as phytoplankton.

Why are seaweeds different colours?

Seaweeds are usually classified according to the colours in their cells. Different coloured seaweeds live in different places in the sea.

Algae contains the green substance **chlorophyll** so that it can make food by photosynthesis, using **energy** from the sun. However, less sunlight reaches deeper water. Green seaweeds are more familiar to us because they grow in shallower waters. Red and brown algae have special colours to help them make food using less light.

Red algae live mostly in deep seawater in warm parts of the world, but some live in shallow rockpools forming chalky crusts around the edges. The largest and toughest algae on Earth are brown algae. Some, like bladderwrack, have air-filled bladders (bubbles) on their **fronds** to help them float.

▲ Giant brown kelp grows up to 60 metres long in the cool waters off California, forming vast underwater forests.

Algae – the key to ocean life

There would be no life in the oceans without algae. Tiny animals eat the billions of tiny single-celled algae floating at sea. Small fish and shrimps eat these animals, and then they become food for larger animals such as big fish, birds and seals.

What are mosses and liverworts?

Have you ever looked at the tiny plants that grow on damp walls and roofs, on rocks near waterfalls or streams, or on fallen trees in woods? Amongst other things, you may have seen green, cushion-shaped plants that feel quite springy if you touch them gently. These are **colonies** (groups) of hundreds or even thousands of tiny moss plants. You may also have seen small, flat green plants that look a bit like mini seaweed. These are liverworts.

Mosses and liverworts are **nonvascular** plants. They make their own food inside their leaves by **photosynthesis,** but have no **phloem** to carry it all around their bodies. Like algae they generally live in damp places, so that all parts of each plant can get the water and **nutrients** it needs to live and grow from its surroundings.

▲ Moss plants usually live in colonies, like this one, because each plant is sheltered better than if it was growing on its own. Also the gaps between each plant in the colony can store more water.

Mosses have small, pointed leaves arranged in spirals around their **stems**. The leaves are not waxy like those of some plants, so mosses can dry out quite quickly in wind or sun as they lose water because of **evaporation**. So, some have hollow **cells** inside that can soak up water to save it for when conditions are dry.

Reproduction

Both mosses and liverworts **reproduce** using **spores**. You may have seen little **stalks** with lumps at the end growing out of moss cushions. The lumps are called **capsules**, which are special boxes that make spores. Moss capsules often have jagged openings (called teeth) that can open when the air is dry and close when it is damp. Spores are blown from a capsule when the teeth are open.

If a moss or liverwort spore falls onto damp ground, it can **germinate** and grow into a new plant. The new plant grows female and male parts that produce **sex cells**. The male sex cells from one moss plant can swim to the female sex cells on another if there is enough water around the plants. If a female sex cell is **fertilized** by a male sex cell, it starts to grow into a new spore capsule on the parent plant.

Some flat liverworts have tiny cups on the top of their leaves. Each cup develops bud-like parts inside, each of which can grow into another liverwort plant identical to its parent.

▼ Liverwort capsules often look like tiny flowers. Special dead cells in the capsule twist and snap as they dry and this flicks the spores out. This liverwort is called *Pelia*.

Types of mosses and liverworts

At first glance most mosses look pretty similar. Remarkably, however, there are around 10,000 **species** of moss in the world! Mosses range in size from the 1-metre-long Brook moss to tiny types best seen under a magnifying glass. Most are less than 10 centimetres high. The easiest way of telling mosses apart is by the arrangement of their leaves or the shape of their **capsules**.

Pollution patrol

Mosses are more sensitive to air pollution than other plants, so they are the first to disappear from a habitat when **pollution** levels begin to rise. This means mosses make great indicators of the amount of pollution there is in the air.

▲ If all the sphagnum moss colonies in the world were added together, they would cover an area the same size as half of the USA.

Where do mosses grow?

Mosses usually grow in damp, sheltered places on the ground or on trees, but some are found in more extreme conditions, from hot **rainforests** to freezing Arctic **tundra**. As many moss species only grow in certain **habitats**, they can also give us clues about what type of soil or rock they are growing on. Sphagnum moss is the name given to several moss species, some green and some red in colour. Sphagnum moss usually grows in cool, wet places called bogs. They grow in **colonies** – some of them massive – around the world.

As sphagnum moss and other bog plants, such as heather, die, they rot slowly in the bog water forming a thick sludge at the bottom. Over long periods of time, more and more plants die and the sludge forms a dense soil called **peat**. People use peat to grow plants on, as it is full of **nutrients**. Peat is also cut into blocks, dried out and burnt as a type of fuel.

Liverworts

There are around 7000 species of liverwort on Earth. They almost always grow in very damp places, but some prefer hot and others cool conditions. Around half of all liverwort species are flat, single leaves held to the ground by rootlets (small **roots**), but the rest look very much like mosses. Liverwort **spores** often **germinate** and form large colonies of plants very quickly after forest fires.

▲ Liverwort leaves.

Medicinal mosses and liverworts

Sphagnum moss is very good at soaking up liquids. During World War I, soldiers and doctors sometimes used moss to dress (cover) wounds as the moss successfully soaked up blood.

Liverworts were given their name because their leaves look a bit like the lobed shape of the human liver. In the past, some people mistakenly believed the shape of plants was a clue to how they could be used as medicine. So liverwort was used to treat liver illness – without any success!

Ferns, horsetails and clubmosses

Ferns are the largest part of one division of the plant **kingdom**. But their division also includes their relatives, the clubmosses and horsetails. These look quite different to ferns, but they have a lot in common with them.

Fern reproduction

Ferns **reproduce** using **spores**. Fern spores are made in cases called **sporangia**. These usually form brown patches on the underside of **fronds**. When spores are ripe, they are released and blow away from the parent plant. If a spore **germinates**, it does not grow into a new fern straight away. First it grows into a tiny green plant-like flap called a **prothallus**. Its job is to produce female and male **sex cells** quickly. Then, in the damp undergrowth, water washes a male sex cell onto a female sex cell. When they join, a new fern plant begins to grow. When it has **roots** and leaves of its own the prothallus dies.

▶ The brown patches on the back of this fern frond are sporangia.

Leaves, stems and roots

All plants in the fern division are **vascular**. They have **stems** and roots with vessels inside to carry water, **nutrients** and sugar. Fern fronds contain **veins** that connect with stem and root vessels. Clubmosses may look like mosses, but like ferns (and unlike mosses) they are vascular. Horsetail stems are hollow and the vessels inside the stems are arranged around the edge. Horsetails have no fronds, but instead have rings of short branches like soft needles spaced along the stem.

Most ferns have special underground parts called **rhizomes**. These look a bit like roots, but they are stems from which roots and shoots grow. In winter, fern fronds die but rhizomes store food that can be used to release **energy** to grow new leaves in spring. Horsetail stems also grow out of rhizomes. Some horsetail stems are green and branched, but others are brown and straight.

▶ Some horsetail stems have swollen ends a bit like very soft **cones**. These are the sporangia, where spores are made.

Wanted – dead or alive

The resurrection plant (*Selaginella*) is a type of clubmoss that lives in places with long seasons of drought. At these times, the plant curls up into a tight brown ball when it dries out. Most people would take it for dead. When rain falls, the plant miraculously comes back to life, uncurling its leaves, which turn green.

Types of ferns

There are around 12,500 different **species** of ferns on Earth. They range in size from tiny plants a few millimetres long, such as mosquito fern (*Azolla*), that live their lives floating on water, to tree ferns up to 20 metres tall in **rainforests**.

▲ On a woodland floor in spring, the first sign of a fern is a strange, green curl that looks like the spiral top of a violin. This is a fern leaf or frond, growing up towards the light. As the frond grows it will uncurl and open out into a long feathery shape.

Different fern species often have names that describe their **frond** shape. Hart's tongue fern (*Phyllitis scolopendrium*) has straight-edged fronds that look a bit like the shape of a hart's (adult male deer's) tongue. The fronds of the shuttlecock fern (*Matteuccia struthiopteris*) are divided into long central **stalks** with lots of leaflets (tiny leaves) arranged down their edges. Each frond looks a bit like a giant feather, so the fern plant looks a bit like the shuttlecock you would use to play badminton with! On the maidenhair fern (*Adiantum*), the **veins** in the leaflets look a bit like a maiden's (girl's) long straight hair.

Tree ferns

There are thousands of tree fern species, many of which live in Australia and New Zealand. The stalks of tree fern fronds grow together to form a tall, thick, hard trunk a bit like that of a palm tree. The scaly tree fern (*Cyathea cooperi*) trunk can grow up to 15 metres tall with fronds up to 6 metres long. Scars on the trunk show where old leaves grew from. **Roots** grow down from the sides of the trunk into the ground for support.

Fern features

Different types of fern fronds have different shaped patches of **sporangia**, which some people mistake for signs of disease. Sometimes the sporangia are arranged in lines of dots or streaks, as in the Hart's tongue fern, but sometimes they are around the edge of each leaflet, as in bracken (*Pteridium*). Royal ferns (*Osmunda regalis*) have sporangia on separate fronds.

Most ferns live in damp soil but some find the growing conditions they need on other plants. Most stag horn ferns (*Platycerium*) are **epiphytes** – their **spores** can **germinate** and grow on the bark high up rainforest trees. Bracken can thrive in dry places as it can spread using underground **rhizomes**.

Types of horsetails and clubmosses

There are around 30 horsetail and 400 clubmoss species on Earth. The largest are around 3 metres high but most are less than 30 centimetres tall. Most grow generally in wet places, and some thrive on ground that contains few **nutrients**. Horsetails and clubmosses are found around the world, but clubmosses are more common in **tropical** countries.

Hard-working horsetail

The scouring rush (*Equisetum hyemale*) is a type of horsetail that makes large amounts of a sharp crystal called silica in its **stems**. In parts of Mexico, bunches of scouring rush are used like sandpaper for polishing wooden furniture.

▼ Some clubmosses, like this *Lycopodium*, have stiff and prickly stems.

What are conifers?

Conifers are trees and shrubs that grow woody or scaly **cones**. Unlike algae, mosses, liverworts and ferns – that all **reproduce** using **spores** – conifers reproduce using **seeds**. Cones contain and protect the seeds as they develop.

Cones versus flowers

Female cones do the same job as flowers – they both make seeds. However, seeds made by a flower form inside a **fruit**, but conifer seeds do not. A few conifers such as juniper have brightly coloured cones shaped like berries. This is to attract animals that eat the flesh and drop the seed away from the parent plant.

Conifers actually have two different types of cones – male and female. Male cones are usually small and make a special dust called **pollen**. Each pollen grain contains male **sex cells**. Female cones are larger and contain female sex cells. In dry weather, breezes blow pollen from male cones onto female cones. If a female sex cell is **fertilized** by a male sex cell, it will grow into an **embryo** inside a seed. Seeds also contain a small food supply that can be used by the embryo to **germinate**. When the seeds are ready, the cones fall or open up to release them.

▼ **The female cones on a Douglas fir are reddish and flower-like. The male cones are yellow and droop like catkins.**

Leaves and trunks

The leaves of most conifers are shaped like needles. Some have scale leaves, which are shaped like the scales on a fish. Their narrow shape and a **waxy** coating help stop conifers from losing water from inside their bodies by **evaporation**. This means they can survive in places that do not provide enough rainfall for broadleaf trees. Most conifers are **evergreen** – when a leaf dies it drops from the tree, but leaves are not all shed at once as they are from **deciduous** trees.

Conifers are **vascular** plants. As they grow bigger they make extra **xylem** vessels, with tough, thick walls. This is called wood. Having tough woody trunks means conifers are strong enough to grow to massive sizes.

▲ Many conifers, like this pine tree, have a special sticky **sap** called **resin** in their trunks. Sap is being collected here.

Cycads and ginkgoes

Conifers have two close relatives that look quite different from them, but also make their seeds in cones. Cycads are evergreen and most look like a cross between a tree fern and a palm tree. Some rely on beetles to carry pollen and have brightly coloured seeds. Ginkgoes are deciduous and have unusual fan-shaped leaves. They can grow up to 30 metres tall. Ginkgo seeds look like yellow cherries and smell like vomit when rotten.

Types of conifers

Many conifers are familiar trees in gardens, parks and forests. Some people even bring one kind – Norway spruce (*Picea abies*) – into their homes at Christmas! Conifers can often be identified by their distinctive shapes, bark, **cones** and needles.

The pine family

Of the 500 different **species** of conifers, over half belong to the pine family. This includes the pines but also the firs (*Abies*), cedars (*Cedrus*), spruces (*Picea*) and larches (*Larix*). Most grow in cold, often mountainous places in northern parts of America, Europe and Asia.

Many spruces and firs grow into large trees in just a few years, so they are often grown for **timber**. However, some pines grow very slowly and can live to great ages. In pines and spruces female cones are often woody, brown and long; in cedars and firs they are shaped like eggs. Pine needles are usually long, narrow and clustered in groups. They contain **resin** that gives them a nice smell.

The secret of eternal youth?

Some bristlecone pines (*Pinus longaeva*) in California, USA, are nearly 5000 years old. So what is their secret? They have very hard, resin-filled wood that cannot be invaded by bugs, and the cold, dry air in the mountains where they live helps preserve them. Although large parts of their trunks die if they are struck by lightning or damaged, tiny strips of living bark can keep them going. Some leaves stay on the trees for up to 45 years.

Southern conifers

The monkey-puzzle (*Araucaria*) and yellow-wood (*Podocarpus*) trees of South America, southern Africa and New Zealand look rather different to other conifers. Monkey-puzzle trees have flat, leathery leaves with sharp points that often grow in spirals along their branches. They have spiky cones that look a bit like tiny hedgehogs!

The yellow-wood family contains 150 species, many that grow in **tropical** places. Most are tall trees, with hard, yellowish wood that makes them very useful for timber. However, one yellow-wood species is a **parasite** – its roots penetrate into another type of yellow-wood and steals its water and **nutrients**! Some yellow-wood conifer trees have broad leaves up to 35 centimetres long that start off red and get greener as they get older.

▲ The branches of a monkey-puzzle tree form an umbrella shape at the top of straight, patterned trunks.

Surprising sequoias

The giant sequoia (*Sequoiadendron giganteum*) of western USA can reach astounding proportions. Some adult trees are 100 metres tall, measure 25 metres around the base, have 50 centimetre-thick bark and **roots** spreading 60 metres on all sides. They can weigh as much as 2000 tonnes – the weight of ten blue whales!

27

What are flowering plants?

The final division in the plant **kingdom** – flowering plants – is by far the largest. It contains **species** that look as different as beech trees and clover. These species are grouped together because they make flowers. The job of all flowers, large or small, is to make **seeds**.

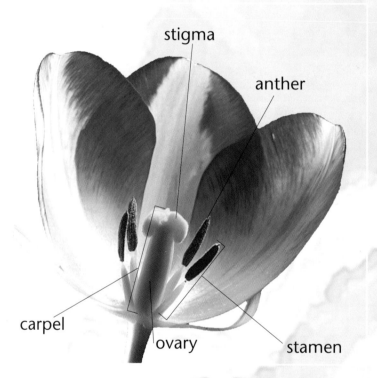

stigma

anther

carpel

ovary

stamen

▲ It is easy to spot the different parts of a flower in a tulip.

Using flowers to make seeds

Flowers contain male and female parts, which both make **sex cells**. Many kinds of plants have both male and female parts in the same flower. Some have separate male and female flowers on the same plant. Others have male and female flowers on separate plants. For a seed to begin to grow, a sex cell from a male part of a flower has to join with a sex cell from a female part.

Flower parts

The male parts of a flower are called **stamens**. The **anthers**, at the top of the stamens, produce the male sex cells, called **pollen**. The female parts of a flower are called the **carpel**. At the bottom of the carpel is the **ovary**, which contains the female sex cells. At the top of each carpel is a sticky pad called a **stigma**. If pollen lands on a stigma it sticks there, and the male sex cell can join with the female sex cell. This is called **fertilization**. The fertilized female sex cell develops into a seed.

◄ As this hummingbird collects nectar from inside this flower, its head is dusted with pollen that will rub off onto the next flower it visits.

Why do flowers look different?

The way a flower gets **pollinated** affects the way it looks. Flowers that rely on animals like insects for pollination have scents and coloured **petals** and **sepals**. These attract the insects, which come to eat sugary **nectar** stored inside the flower. When insect visitors reach for a flower's nectar, they accidentally pick up pollen. When they visit another flower, the pollen is rubbed off onto the stigma.

Flowers that rely on wind for pollination tend to be much less colourful. They do not need bright colours, sweet scents and food to attract insects. Their anthers and stigmas stick out from the flower so the wind can blow their pollen away.

From flower to fruit

As seeds develop, the ovary around them grows into a **fruit** and the other flower parts die. Fruits protect seeds and help to move them to new ground where they can **germinate**. The smell and taste of fleshy fruits attract animals, which eat the flesh and then spit out the seeds or deposit them in their droppings. Some flowering plants, such as sycamore, have dry fruits shaped like wings to carry their seeds on the wind. Others, such as burdock, have fruits covered with tiny hooks that catch onto an animal's fur and are moved.

Classifying flowering plants

Nine out of every ten **species** of plant on Earth are flowering plants. With such a variety of plants to work with, scientists have come up with lots of ways of classifying different flowering plants.

Classifying by features

Flowering parts can be grouped by the many different features and characteristics that we can see. They can be sorted according to leaf shape. For instance, trees with five-pointed leaves belong to the maple family. They can be sorted by the shape or form of their flower. For example, flowers with a boat-shaped **petal** – containing the **carpel** and **stamens** – and two 'roof' petals above are from the pea family. Trees could be grouped by the shape their branches usually grow in or by their different kinds of **bark**.

Life cycles

Flowering plants can also be divided according to how they live their lives. Many are **annuals** – they make flowers and die in one growing season and their **seeds germinate** the following year. Others are **biennials** – they grow and then die back in one season, but their **roots** survive over winter and fuel the growth of a new plant the following year. **Perennials** survive for many years without dying back completely each year.

▲ Flowers in the pea family have five petals and often look similar. These are everlasting pea (*Lathyrus latifolius*).

Monocots and dicots

One of the most important ways that scientists classify flowering plants has to do with the number of **cotyledons** inside the plant's **seeds**. Cotyledons, which are also known as seed leaves, are food stores that help the **embryo** inside the seed to grow. Flowering plants either have one or two cotyledons inside each seed. If they have one cotyledon they are called monocotyledons (or **monocots**). If they have two cotyledons they are called dicotyledons (or **dicots**).

As you usually cannot look inside a seed, there are other ways to tell monocots and dicots apart. In monocots, such as tulips, **veins** are usually arranged in parallel lines along the length of the leaves. In dicots, such as maple, the leaves usually have one or several large veins with little ones branching off them.

▼ Monocots such as grasses have parallel veins in their leaves, but dicots, such as this maple, have branched veins in their leaves.

Types of flowering plants

Of over 250,000 **species** of flowering plants, about one-fifth are **monocots**, including irises, onions and lilies. The grass family of monocots is probably the most familiar to us. There are around 10,000 species in the grass family, including vital cereal crops, such as wheat, rice and corn, the hardy grasses that make up sport pitches and bamboos so strong they can be used to make buildings. Grasses are very quick-growing plants, with tough but flexible **stems**, similar to their relatives the rushes and sedges.

Awesome orchids

The orchids are an even bigger family of monocots, with nearly 20,000 species. Their flowers are very distinctive, with colourful, unusually shaped lower **petals**. Some are **tropical** vines like the vanilla orchid, which has **seed pods** that are used for flavouring food. Many are small plants that live in soil in colder places, but most are **epiphytes** in **rainforests**. Epiphyte orchids get closer to the sunlight above the trees by growing on the trees than they could on the dark forest floor. Instead of growing underground, their **roots** hang in the humid air to absorb moisture.

Exotic monocots

Some of the most familiar monocot trees include the coconut palm (*Cocas nucifera*) of tropical beaches and the date palms (*Phoenix dactylifera*) of hot deserts. The ginger family contains several important and familiar tropical monocot plants, such as banana (*Musa*), ginger (*Zingiber officinale*), and bird-of-paradise (*Strelitzia reginae*) flower.

▶ **The flowers of the ginger plant.**

Dynamic dicots

The biggest group of flowering plants are the **dicots**. Around 190,000 species of flowering plants are dicots. This plant group contains the tiny wolffia duckweed, whose flowers are the size of a full stop on this page, right up to the Australian eucalyptus trees, which reach a height of 100 metres.

The largest dicot families are the sunflowers and the peas. The 24,000 members of the sunflower family mostly have compound flowers – flower heads containing lots of small flowers (or florets). Some, like olive and coffee, are large trees or shrubs, but others, like daisies, thistles and chrysanthemums, are very small plants. The **legume** family (peas and beans) contains mostly plants such as beans, lentils and groundnuts, which make their seeds in dry **fruit** called pods.

No family resemblance?

Scientists try to group plants based on how closely they are related – that is, how recently they shared a common **ancestor**. Sometimes they find close relationships between unlikely plants. The euphorbia family of dicots contains not only the poinsettia plants given as gifts in winter, but also cactus-like spurges, because both have special cup-shaped flowers containing separate **anthers** and one or several **carpels** on a **stalk**.

▲ Water lilies, like this one, are dicots. They grow and live on the edge of ponds and lakes, in shallow water.

The success of flowering plants

Flowering plants are found in almost every part of the planet, except the oceans. They live in **habitats** as different as windswept mountains, lush grasslands, marshes and bogs, dense forests, hot and cold deserts and rushing rivers.

Adapt to survive

Some **species** of flowering plant can grow in several different habitats, but most are specially **adapted** to life in one particular habitat. This means that over thousands or millions of years the plants have changed and developed a shape, size and **life cycle** that is ideally suited to the place where they grow. For example, cacti have adapted to life in hot, dry deserts by having thick, fleshy **stems** that can store water and thin, spiny leaves to reduce the amount of water lost by **evaporation**.

▲ Flowering plants are so successful they even manage to live in some of the coldest places on Earth, such as Alaska.

Tree tactics

Trees have developed ways of surviving in their different habitats. In colder climates, **deciduous** trees drop their leaves in autumn so they are not damaged during cold winters. New leaves grow in spring. In monsoon climates, deciduous trees shed their leaves at the start of the dry season and grow new ones when monsoon rains come. In countries with warm summers, cold winters and light rain all year, some **evergreen** trees have no need to lose their leaves.

Plant partnerships

One reason flowering plants are so successful is because of their ability to use other **organisms** to help them grow and **reproduce**. For example, many flowering plants succeed by relying on particular animals for **pollination**. One orchid species has a long flower whose **nectar** (and **pollen**) can only be reached by a moth with a 30-centimetre-long tongue. Each of the 1000 different species of **tropical** fig tree needs a different wasp to pollinate their flowers.

Fungi friends

Many flowering plants rely on **fungi** and **bacteria** in the places they grow. This is because fungi and bacteria help break down plants and animals that have died, releasing **nutrients**. Each tree species in a wood may rely on a massive underground **colony** of just one species of fungi to supply its nutrients.

Feeding off others

Parasitic flowering plants, such as rafflesia, have **roots** that grow into the parts of other plants and steal the nutrients and food they need from them. **Carnivorous** plants, such as sundews, 'eat' insects. They catch insects in trap- or tube-shaped leaves, then digest them using special juices.

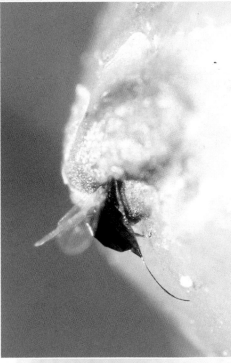

▲ **Wasp entering fig fruit.**

Fig nurseries

Figs and wasps help each other. Female wasps can only pollinate fig flowers – which are hidden inside what we think of as the **fruit** – if she lays her eggs on them. The fig then protects the growing wasps, until they hatch and fly off.

Plants: then and now

We know that dinosaurs once lived on Earth because of the **fossil** bones that have been found. We can imagine their lives in the past by studying the lives of their close relatives today, the lizards. Plant fossils give us similar clues about plants of the past.

Evolution

Since the first plants appeared on Earth, continents have moved, oceans have become smaller and temperatures have changed. Some plants could not survive these changes and they became extinct (died out). Others survived because they were stronger in some way. These plants **reproduced** and had offspring with more of the features that made their parents successful. Over millions of years, new plants developed. This is called **evolution**. New **species** continue to evolve as **habitats** on Earth continue to change.

Like any fossils, they cannot tell the whole story. Not everything that ever died on Earth has become a fossil – some **organisms** just rot away. However, if one plant fossil is in an older rock than another, it means it appeared on Earth first. From studying fossils we know what the first plants were, living in the sea thousands of millions of years ago. They were very similar to the algae of today.

▶ These are fossil horsetail plants that lived hundreds of millions of years ago. The horsetails of today look very similar to the ancient plants, but they are a lot smaller – some early horsetails were 30 metres tall!

Plant evolution

As large areas of land emerged from the sea, some early plants were washed ashore. Many died, but some survived in the drier conditions because they had thicker skins. Over time, mosses and liverworts evolved. Then, as now, these plants could only live in damp places as they reproduce by **spores** that **germinate** in water.

Other plants evolved into ferns and horsetails. They could grow taller as they had **roots** and vessels to move water and food through their bodies, but they still needed wet conditions for spore germination. Much later, conifers evolved. Conifers reproduce using **seeds**. Seeds need less water to grow than spores, so conifers spread to drier places. Conifers covered the Earth 250–300 million years ago.

Later, flowering plants evolved. They used wind and the abundant insect life for **pollination**. Their developing seeds were protected and moved around by **fruits**, and each seed was packaged with the food it needed to germinate. These developments made reproduction in flowering plants rapid and successful, and today they are the most widespread plants on Earth.

Fossil records

The oldest plant fossils are of algae that lived nearly 3500 million years ago. Earliest mosses appeared about 450 million years ago; ferns, horsetails and conifers had all appeared by 250–300 million years ago. The first flowering plants appeared about 150 million years later.

◄ A fossil of an early flower, found in Wyoming, USA.

Studying plants

In the past, botanists (plant scientists) often studied plants by picking what looked interesting or rare and taking it home to look at. There were several problems with this. They killed the plant and it often rotted before they got it home; once they removed it from where it grew they could not see how it fitted into its **habitat**.

It is better to look at, write notes about, draw or photograph the plant in its habitat and then compare and confirm this information using specimens (samples) kept in museums or botanical gardens. If botanists of today need to collect a specimen to study it, they have better means of preservation, such as refrigerators, than in the past, and they can travel much more easily and quickly.

▲ As it is still easier to pick rare orchids than grow them from **seed**, many **species**, such as this flame of the forest orchid (*Butea frondosa*), have become **endangered**.

The orchid hunters

Orchids became so popular about 250 years ago that rich people hired professional orchid hunters to find new types. The hunters risked death from snake bites, disease and falling out of trees as they attempted to reach unusual **epiphyte** varieties that were tens of metres above ground in tropical rainforests. Some types became so prized that they were sold for hundreds of thousands of pounds!

Has plant collecting helped us?

Plant collectors have changed the way our world looks and how it feeds and cures itself. European collectors brought back rhododendrons from Asia to fill their gardens and potatoes from South America to fill their stomachs. Much European and American wealth came from the sale of sugar, cocoa, spices and cotton crops grown and tended by slaves in **tropical** countries. Plant medicines used by local people in tropical countries have been collected and used worldwide.

Counting on classification

Although hundreds of thousands of plant species have been identified, some botanists estimate that in the lush tropical **rainforests** there are many thousands more waiting to be discovered! By classifying plants in the world we can not only identify the different species we know of and work out how they may have evolved in the past, we can also recognize new species, some of which may be useful to us.

By protecting and studying plants and how they live in their habitats, we can understand better how the lives of all living things on Earth are connected. Classification can then benefit not only those on Earth now, but also future generations who will live here.

▶ **In virtually unexplored parts of the rainforest there may be new medicinal plants that can cure diseases such as cancer.**

Try it yourself!

Classification practice

Classification is all about sorting and grouping. You can classify just about anything, but it is good to start with a simple exercise.

You will need:
- 8 different objects (e.g. button, shell, stone, pencil, eraser)
- a large sheet of paper
- a pencil or pen.

With the paper lying on its side, draw one big circle in the middle at the top, then two arrows leading to two circles below that. Put the objects into the big circle. Now divide the objects into two groups. You can divide them in different ways: by size (large or small), or whether found or bought. Make a note of what way you used to divide them up.

Put the two groups into two circles drawn at the top of the paper. Then subdivide each group into two smaller groups using a different way, for instance by colour or by shape – again, note down how you divided them.

Repeat this process again until you have each object in its own circle. You should also, by now, have a list of the different ways you divided the objects up at each step.

Now start the process again, but this time mix up the different ways of dividing the objects up and see if you end up with the same groups. Often you will not and this shows how tricky classification can be!

This is a bit like the way plants are classified. The smallest circles are a bit like **species'** names, the next largest circles are like **genus** names and so on. Scientists don't just use shape, size and colour to classify plants. They also use leaf and flower shape, arrangements of leaves on branches, whether or not a plant makes **seeds** or **spores**, and many other different ways.

Monocot or dicot?

Flowering plants are usually divided into two groups depending on whether they have:

- one or two seed leaves (food stores), called **cotyledons**, inside their seeds
- parallel (side by side) **veins** or veins in a branched arrangement in their leaves.

Have a go at classifying **monocots** and **dicots** yourself.

You will need:

- a few roasted peanuts in shells
- a small tin of sweetcorn
- grass seeds
- cress seeds
- 2 saucers
- 2 circles of blotting paper
- 2 clear plastic pots that fit over the saucers
- a magnifying glass.

One or two parts?

Break open some peanut shells, rub off the brown skins and examine the peanuts. These are dicots; the two cotyledons are the two halves of each peanut.

Get an adult to open the tin of sweetcorn and examine some of the corn kernels. Pinch off the yellow seed coat. A corn seed is a monocot; it is in one piece.

One or two seed leaves?

Put each piece of paper onto one saucer and moisten the paper with water. Then sprinkle cress seeds on one and grass seeds on the other. Put a plastic pot over the top of each saucer and carefully put them in a sunny place, out of the way (perhaps a windowsill). When the seeds have **germinated**, have a look at the leaves that first come out of the seed cases using the magnifying glass.

Cress is a dicot and you should see two mini-leaves emerge from the cress seeds. Grass is a monocot and you should only be be able to see one leaf emerge from each grass seed.

41

Looking at plant classification

The plant **kingdom** is usually divided up into five divisions. Most plants make their own food by **photosynthesis** using a green chemical called **chlorophyll**. This makes most plants look green. However, some plants contain other chemicals that mask the chlorophyll making them look a different colour. Plants also cannot move from place to place on their own like animals.

Classification is tricky and not everyone agrees on a single system. For example, because algae are different from most other plants, some scientists classify them in a kingdom called Protoctista, which also contains microscopic **organisms** that can move in water.

Algae:
- range in size from simple single **cells** or short chains of cells to more complex giant seaweeds
- live in water or very damp places; most live in seawater
- are **nonvascular**
- **reproduce** using **spores** made in swellings on leaf-like fronds
- have no **roots**; many have **holdfasts** to anchor themselves
- are a food source of marine food chains.

There are about 12,000 **species** of algae. They divide into three groups within the algae division: red algae, e.g. carragheen, green algae, e.g. sea lettuce and brown algae, e.g. giant kelp.

Mosses and liverworts:
- are small, green land plants, that often grow in **colonies**
- usually live in damp places, from bogs to soil to tree bark
- are nonvascular
- reproduce using spores made in **capsules**
- have root-like rhizoids to anchor.

There are about 24,000 species of mosses and liverworts.

Ferns, horsetails and clubmosses:

- are green land plants that vary in size, from small to large
- are **vascular**
- reproduce using spores which are made in spore sacs (**sporangia**) on undersides of leaves in ferns or on cone-shaped sporangia at ends of stems in horsetails, and on special groups of leaves in clubmosses
- have large **frond**-like fern leaves that unwind and expand as they grow
- typically spread using underground stems (**rhizomes**).

There are about 12,500 species of ferns, horsetails and clubmosses.

Conifers:

- vary in size, from small shrubs to enormous trees
- usually have needle-like leaves, and are usually **evergreen**
- are vascular
- reproduce using **seeds** made in **cones**
- have two types of cone: wind carries **pollen** from male cone to female cone where a seed develops from **fertilized** ovule.

There are 500 species of conifer, divided into three groups: conifers, e.g. pines (*pinus*), cycads, e.g. sago palm (*Cycas revoluta*) and ginkgoes, represented by one species *Ginkgo biloba*.

Flowering plants:

- vary immensely in size (from tiny aquatic plants to large trees) and form (from cacti to grasses)
- are the dominant vegetation on Earth, growing in most **habitats**
- usually have well-defined leaves, **stems** and roots
- are vascular, with complex **xylem** and **phloem** tissue
- reproduce using seeds made in flowers
- have flowers with male **stamens** and female **carpels**; the pollen is carried from stamens to carpels by animal **pollinators**, wind or water
- have seeds that develop inside **fruit**

There are over 250,000 species of flowering plant, divided into two major groups: **monocots**, e.g. grasses, and **dicots**, e.g. oak trees.

Glossary

adapt change over thousands of years to fit in with a habitat

ancestors earlier generations of organisms (living things). For example, your great-grandparents and your grandparents are your ancestors.

annual plant that grows, flowers, makes seeds and dies all within one year (or season)

anther top part of the male part of a flower (stamen) where pollen is found in pollen sacs

bacteria tiny organisms in the soil, water and air

biennial plant that lives for two years. It usually flowers, makes seeds and dies in the second year.

capsule container of spores found at the end of stalks on certain plants

carbon dioxide gas in the air which plants use for photosynthesis

carnivorous plant or animal that eats parts of insects or other animals

carpel name for the female parts of a flower. The ovary, style and stigma together make up a carpel.

cells building blocks of living things

chlorophyll green substance found in plants that is used in photosynthesis

colonies groups of similar plants that take over an area of land

cone form of dry fruit (in which seeds develop) produced by conifer trees

consumer organism that needs to consume (eat) plants or the animals that eat plants in order to live

cotyledon food stores that help the embryo inside the seed to grow

deciduous trees that lose all their leaves at much the same time

dicot type of plant that has two seed leaves (cotyledon) inside each of its seeds, which act as food stores

embryo a plant embryo is a very young plant contained in a seed

endangered when a plant or animal is in danger of dying out

energy ability in living things to do what they need to do in order to live and grow. Plants and animals get the energy they need from their food.

epiphyte plant that grows on another plant for support

evaporation when water turns from liquid into a vapour (a gas)

evergreen plants that do not lose all their leaves at once, but lose some and grow new ones all year round

evolution way new kinds of plants and animals come into being as a result of many small changes that happen over thousands of years

fertilize/fertilization when a male sex cell and a female sex cell fuse (join together) and begin to form a seed

fossil preserved remains of a plant (or animal) that lived millions of years ago

frond leaf-like part of plants such as ferns or seaweeds

fruit part of a plant that contains and protects its seeds

fungi group of living things that cannot make their own food by photosynthesis, e.g. mushrooms

genes genes control how an organism looks, how it will survive, grow and change through its life

genus in Linnaeus's double (or Latin) name system, a general (group) name

germinate/germination when a seed starts to grow

habitat place where plants or animals live

holdfasts root-like part of a plant such as seaweed that it uses to hold onto a rock. Holdfasts are not roots.

kingdom in classification, the largest group that living things belong to

legume name for a family of plants that all grow their seeds inside pods. Peas and beans are types of legumes.

life cycle order of events in the life of an organism

monocot type of plant that has one seed leaf (cotyledon) inside each seed, which acts as a food store

nectar sugary liquid plants make to attract insects, which like to eat it

nonvascular term to describe plants that do not have tubes for transporting fluids

nutrient kind of chemical that nourishes plants and animals, keeping them healthy

organism living thing, such as a bacterium, cell, plant or animal

ovary rounded bottom part of the carpel, contains the female sex cell

ovule plant's female sex cell

oxygen gas in the air and gas which plants release into the air during the process of photosynthesis

parasite/parasitic plant (or animal) that lives on and gets its food from another living thing

peat partly rotted remains of plants such as bog moss

perennial plant that lives for more than two years, often for many years

petals usually the largest and most colourful parts of a flower

phloem tubes that carry food (sugars) made in the leaf to all the other parts of the plant

photosynthesis process by which plants make their own food using water, carbon dioxide (a gas in the air) and energy from sunlight

plankton microscopic organisms, that live in the surface waters of the oceans

pod capsule (container) that holds the seeds of legume plants, such as peas

pollen tiny, dust-like particles produced by a flower, which contain the plant's male sex cells

pollinate/pollination when pollen travels from the anthers of one flower to the stigma of the same or a different flower

pollinator insect or animal that carries pollen from one flower to another

pollution when something poisons or harms any part of the environment (the natural world)

producer organism that produces its own food within itself

prothallus tiny plant-like organism that grows from a spore. A fern prothallus can produce a new fern plant.

rainforest kind of forest that exists in very hot and wet (rainy) countries of the world

reproduce/reproduction when a living thing produces young like itself

resin special kind of sticky sap that flows just beneath a tree's layer of bark

rhizomes special kind of stem, which grows under the ground instead of up in the air

roots plant parts that anchor a plant firmly in the ground and take in water and nutrients

sap sugary fluid containing food made in the leaves. Sap flows in a plant's phloem tubes.

sepal green petal-like structure. Sepals protect the inner parts of a bud until the bud is ready to open.

sex cells plants make these in their sexual (male or female) parts

species group of living things that are similar in many ways and can reproduce together

sporangia sacs or capsules containing groups of spores

spores tiny particles, usually containing a single cell, that can grow into a new plant

stalks part of the plant that attaches the leaf to the stem. Flower stalks attach little flowers to a stem.

stamen male reproductive part of a flower, which produces pollen

stem part of the plant that holds it upright and supports its leaves and flowers

stigma part of the flower that receives pollen in the process of pollination. Stigmas are usually found at the top of a stalk, called the style.

timber wood that has been cut from a tree to be used for building or furniture-making

tropical area of the world around the Equator which has the hottest climate on Earth

tundra name for areas in the Arctic regions of the world that are only free from snow and ice for a few months of the year

vascular term to describe plants that have xylem and phloem tubes for transporting water, nutrients and food to the various parts of their body

vein tiny tube that supports a leaf. Xylem and phloem tubes run through the veins, carrying water to the leaves and foods from them to other parts of the plant.

xylem tubes in a plant that carry water and nutrients from the roots to all the other parts of the plant

Find out more

Books

Eyewitness Guides: Plant and *Tree*, David Burnie, (Dorling Kindersley, 1988)

How to Identify Trees, Patrick Harding and Gill Tomblin (Collins, 1998)

Kingfisher Field Guide to the Plant Life of Britain and Europe, Michael Chinery (Kingfisher, 1987)

The Oxford Children's Encyclopedia of Plants and Animals (OUP, 2000)

Plants, Jo Ellen Moore (Evan-Moor Educational Publishers, 1986)

The Private Life of Plants, David Attenborough (BBC Books, 1995)

Spotter's Guide to Wild Plants, Sue Jacquemier and Patricia Monahan (Usborne, 1987)

The Visual Dictionary of Plants, Deni Brown (Dorling Kindersley, 1992)

The Wildlife Trust's Guide to Wild Flowers, N. Hammond (ed.) (New Holland Publishers, 2002)

World of Plants, L. Howell and K. Rogers (Usborne, 2001)

Websites

www.bbc.co.uk/nature/plants/
The BBCi nature site features a gardening calendar, fun facts and links to Private Life of Plants information based on TV series presented by Sir David Attenborough.

www.edenproject.com/3772.htm
At the Eden project website, you can find lots of information about the remarkable Eden greenhouses, where different plant habitats have been created, plus an interesting plant quiz.

www.foe.co.uk/campaigns/biodiversity

www.wwf.org.uk/core/wildlife/fs_0000000 029.asp
These conservation sites provide information on dangers facing wild plants and habitats, and what Friends of the Earth and the World Wide Fund for Nature are doing to help them survive.

mbgnet.mobot.org/index.htm
At Missouri Botanical Garden's website, you can compare the habitats of the world.

www.news.wisc.edu/titanarum/index.html
A website devoted to the blooming of the titan arum – one of the world's most remarkable flowers. Here you can see its bud opening!

www.urbanext.uiuc.edu/gpe/gpe.html
Great Plant Escape is a fun way of learning about what different plant parts do. This website also supplies a simple glossary of terms.

Places to visit

Many museums, arboretums (botanical garden devoted to trees) and botanic gardens are fascinating places to visit. You could try:

The Royal Botanical Gardens, Kew, near London

Westonbirt Arboretum, Gloucestershire

Eden Project, St Austell, Cornwall

You can also find out about plants by visiting local garden centres.

Index

Titles in the *Life of Plants* series include:

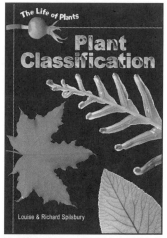

Hardback   0 431 11883 3

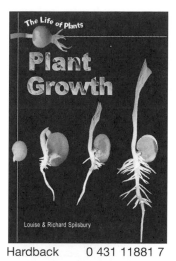

Hardback   0 431 11881 7

Hardback   0 431 11884 1

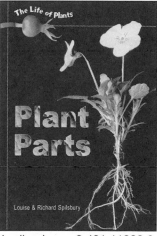

Hardback   0 431 11880 9

Hardback   0 431 11885 X

Hardback   0 431 11882 5

Find out about the other titles in this series on our website www.heinemann.co.uk/library